BIGGEST

AND

smallest

Written by
Camilla de la Bédoyère

QEB Publishing

Designed & edited by Starry Dog Books Ltd
Picture research: Starry Dog Books Ltd

Consultant: Dr Gerald Legg,
Booth Museum of Natural History, Brighton

Copyright © QEB Publishing, Inc. 2010

Published in the United States by
QEB Publishing, Inc.
3 Wrigley, Suite A
Irvine, CA 92618

www.qed-publishing.co.uk

Library of Congress Cataloging-in-Publication Data
De la Bédoyère, Camilla.
  Biggest and smallest / Camilla de la Bédoyère.
    p. cm. -- (QEB Animal opposites)
Includes index.
  ISBN 978-1-59566-789-2 (library binding)
  1. Body size--Juvenile literature. 2. Animals--Juvenile
literature. I. Title.
  QL799.3.D425 2011
  590--dc22
                        2010010661

ISBN 978 159566 789 2

Printed in China

Picture credits

Key: t = top, b = bottom, l = left, r = right, c = centre,
FC = front cover, BC = back cover.

A = Alamy, C = Corbis, FLPA = Frank Lane Picture Agency,
G = Getty Images, IQM = imagequestmarine.com,
NPL = Nature Picture Library (naturepl.com),
PL = Photolibrary, PS = Photoshot, S = shutterstock.com.

FC l S/ © Kletr, FC r S/ © Al Mueller; BC bl S/ © Eric
Isselée, BC tl, tr, br S/ © Picsfive.

1l S/ © Christian Musat, 1r S/ © Eric Isselée;
2 S/ © Mogens Trolle; 3t S/ © Peter Wollinga; 4l
IQM/ © Peter Batson, 4r S/ © pandapaw; 5l S/
© Eric Isselée, 5r Dr Daniel Kronauer, Harvard
University; 6t S/ © Torsten Lorenz, 6b S/ ©
Christian Musat; 7t S/ © Mogens Trolle, 7b S/
© Andreas Meyer; 8 S/ © Stephen Inglis; 9t S/ ©
Alan Merrigan, 9b PL (Juniors Bildarchiv); 10t S/
© Dominique Capelle, 10b S/ © Attila Jándi; 11
PL (OSF)/ © Rafi Ben-Shahar; 12 PS (NHPA)/ ©
Martin Harvey, 12b S/ © Dennis Donohue; 13t A/
© David Osborn, 13bl A/ © Lee Dalton, 13br S/
© Eric Isselée; 14t PS/ © Gerald Cubitt, 14b S/ ©
Nickolay Khoroshkov; 15t S/ © Jaana Piira, 15b
S/ © Jerry Sharp; 16t S/ © fivespots, 16b IQM/ ©
James D. Watt; 17t NPL/ © Nick Garbutt, 17b
IQM/ © Scott Tuason; 18c IQM/ © Jez Tryner,
18b FLPA (Minden Pictures)/ © Norbert Wu; 19t
IQM/ © Peter Parks, 19b IQM/ © James D. Watt;
20b C/ © Michael & Patricia Fogden, 20-21 G/ ©
Peter David; 21t S/ © KRCrowley, 21b S/ © Eric
Isselée; 22t IQM/ © Johnny Jensen, 22b S/ © Morten
Hilmer; 23t S/ © Ewan Chesser, 23b S/ © Le Do;
24-25 C/ © Denis Scott, 24b IQM/ © Peter Parks;
25t S/ © Lijuan Guo, 25b IQM/ © Peter Parks; 26c
S/ © Peter Wollinga, 26b S/ © Eric Isselée; 27 S/ ©
worldswildlifewonders; 28l S/ © Debra James, 28r
S/ © Photobank; 29tl S/ © Linn Currie, 29tr S/ ©
Martin Maritz, 29cr S/ © Katrina Brown, 29br S/ ©
Tischenko Irina; 32 S/ © Morten Hilmer.

The words in **bold** are
explained in the glossary
on page 30.

Contents

Big and Small

Life is tough in the animal world. Sometimes being big can help you to survive, and sometimes being small works best.

More **complex animals** with big brains, such as elephants, tend to be bigger than the simpler animals, such as starfish and spiders.

4

The no. 1 tallest animal

RECORD BREAKER is the ...

GIRAFFE

Giraffes are the tallest animals in the world. Their great height helps them to reach into trees and feed on leaves that smaller animals can't reach. Giraffes can be 20 feet (6 meters) tall.

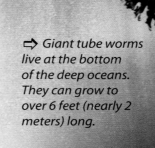

⇨ *Giant tube worms live at the bottom of the deep oceans. They can grow to over 6 feet (nearly 2 meters) long.*

Who's cleverest?

However, there are no hard-and-fast rules in the **animal kingdom**. Little pygmy marmosets grow to just 6 inches (15 centimeters) long, but they are very clever monkeys. Giant tube worms are thirteen times larger than pygmy marmosets, but they have no proper brain at all.

⇨ *Little pygmy marmosets can leap and dart between trees, using their tail for balance. They live in the rainforests of South America.*

ACTUAL ‹‹‹ SIZE ›››

Driver ants are giants in the bug world. The queen is 2 inches (50 millimeters) long. She grows so big because she has to produce millions of eggs each month. The world's smallest ants (*Carebara* ants) measure just 0.03 inches (0.8 millimeters) long.

Driver ants with their queen

in 1   2   3   4

Is Big Best?

What is best about being big? For one thing, it means most hunters will think twice before attacking you.

⬇ *White rhinos are actually gray. They live in Africa and can grow to 13 feet (4 meters) long.*

Rhino's eye

6

ACTUAL ««« SIZE »»»

Rhinos have surprisingly small eyes for their great size. These grazers rely more on their sense of smell to detect danger.

⇓ Lions usually hunt animals that are smaller or weak. When they hunt in a group, they may attack larger prey.

A rhino is the size of a small car and is covered in thick skin. It is simply too large for most big cat **predators**, such as cheetahs or lions. If a big cat did attack one of these mighty beasts, it would stand a good chance of being squashed underfoot and stabbed by the rhino's horn.

Advantages of size

Being big makes some animals, such as lions and bears, better hunters—they are more easily able to defeat other, smaller animals. Being large has another advantage, too. It helps a body to stay at a steady temperature, and this allows the animal to save energy. Animals that have a tiny body, such as the common shrew, lose heat quickly.

The no. 1 biggest land animal **RECORD BREAKER** is ...
SAUROPOSEIDON

Although big bodies can support big brains, it isn't always the case. The dinosaur *Sauroposeidon* was the largest land animal ever to have lived. It stood an incredible 59 feet (18 meters) tall, but its head was very small in relation to its body.

7

Small to Survive

Most of the world's animals are much smaller than us. There may be as many as 30 million species, or types, of animal. Of these, at least 9.8 million are smaller than your hand!

Invertebrates are animals without backbones, such as worms and beetles. Backbones and bony skeletons hold a big body up. Since invertebrates don't have this support, they are mostly small.

⇦ *Most praying mantids are long, green and glossy— just like leaves. They can hide among plants, and pounce upon other small animals.*

ACTUAL <<< SIZE >>>

Goliath bird-eating spider

Most spiders, even small ones, are equipped to kill their prey with deadly **venom**. One of the biggest spiders is the Goliath bird-eating spider, which is about the size of a dinner plate! Its legspan can be nearly 12 inches (30 centimeters).

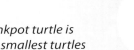

in 1 2 3

A neat package

Being small—whether you are a mini moth or a tiny turtle—means you may have some advantages over bigger beasts. You can probably hide better, you don't take up much space, you can eat less, and you don't have to spend years growing big enough to mate and have young.

9

⬇ *The stinkpot turtle is one of the smallest turtles in the world. It measures about 2 to 5 inches (5 to 12 centimeters) long, and makes a foul smell when it is scared!*

Curious Cousins

When a male African elephant walks up to you, there is no doubt that you are face to face with one of nature's giants.

An elephant can measure 30 feet (9 meters) from trunk tip to tail tip and weigh more than 13,200 pounds (6000 kilograms). This makes it the world's largest land animal.

Fur in the family

Strangely, the elephant's closest cousin seems to be a furry little **mammal** called a hyrax. There is not much of a family likeness!

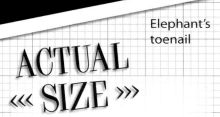

Elephant's toenail

ACTUAL «« SIZE »»

Elephants can talk to each other using their feet. They make low rumbling noises, which other elephants feel as vibrations that travel through the ground and into the soles of their feet.

Tell-tale bones

Scientists think that elephants and hyraxes are related because the bones in their feet and teeth are very similar. They also both live very long lives— elephants usually to about 60 years and hyraxes to 15 years.

⇦ *Rock hyraxes live among rocks and like to sunbathe.*

11

⇐ *African elephants are the largest of all elephants. They have much bigger ears than Asian elephants. An elephant's tusks are teeth that can grow to 10 feet (3 meters) long.*

Feathered Friends

⇩ Ostriches live in the grasslands of Africa.

Birds come in all shapes and sizes, from the mighty ostrich to the miniature bee hummingbird.

12

All birds have feathers, but not all of them fly. The world's largest birds are built for speed on land. They are simply too heavy to fly.

The no. 1 biggest owl **RECORD BREAKER** is the ...
EURASIAN EAGLE OWL

The Eurasian eagle owl is the largest of all owls, with a record-breaking wingspan of 6.5 feet (2 meters). The females are bigger than the males.

Long legs

An ostrich stands about 6.5 feet (2 meters) tall. When it runs, it can cover more than 16 feet (5 meters) in one giant stride. Its small wings are no good for flying, so when an ostrich senses danger, it has to run fast or kick its attacker.

⇐ *Albatrosses fly long distances over the ocean to reach land, where they make their nests and lay their eggs.*

ACTUAL SIZE »»»

The bee hummingbird measures just over 2 inches (57 millimeters) long, including its tail and bill. It is the world's smallest bird, and is easily mistaken for a bee. Weighing a fraction of an ounce, it is so light that you wouldn't feel it resting on your hand. The whole bird is about the same size as an ostrich's eye!

Expert gliders

Albatrosses have huge wings, useful for gliding on warm **air currents** high in the sky. The wandering albatross has the largest wingspan of any bird. Its wings measure 138 inches (350 centimeters) from tip to tip.

Ostrich's eye

Bee hummingbird

in 1 2 3 4

Social Climbers

Apes, monkeys, and lemurs are primates. They like to live in family groups, and their bodies are perfect for climbing trees, where they find fruit to eat.

14

⇧ *Pygmy mouse lemurs rarely come down from the trees. Their large eyes help them see well in the dark.*

⇐ *Large male gorillas are called silverbacks, because their fur turns gray as they age. One silverback is in charge of each gorilla family, and he protects them.*

People used to think that gorillas were a type of monster, but now we know they are gentle giants—and apes, like us. Gorillas are the largest primates. They are so big that they spend most of their time on the ground, but even the "big daddies" occasionally climb high up a tree to fetch ripe, tasty fruit. If they feel threatened, gorillas use their great size to scare away other animals, and humans, too.

15

Nifty movers

The pygmy mouse lemur is the world's smallest primate. It is only 2.4 inches (6 centimeters) long, but its tail adds another 5 inches (13 centimeters). Pygmy mouse lemurs live in the forests of Madagascar. Being small means they can scuttle swiftly through branches at night, searching for insects, flowers, and fruit.

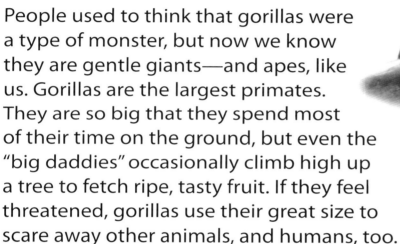

ACTUAL ‹‹‹ SIZE ›››

Gorillas have hands that are very similar to ours. Each large hand has four fingers, a thumb, and fingernails. Gorillas can use their hands to grip, hold, twist, and open things, too.

A gorilla's fingernail

in 1   2   3   4

Scary Reptiles

Millions of years ago, reptiles were the largest animals ever to have lived. In the long run, being big did not help them survive.

Today's reptiles are much smaller than the dinosaurs. But that doesn't mean you would want to come face to face with them! The Komodo dragon is a large lizard. It can grow to nearly 10 feet (3 meters) long and is famous for being fast on its feet, aggressive and having a deadly bite.

The no. 1 scary reptile **RECORD BREAKER** is the ...

RETICULATED PYTHON

Snakes are reptiles, too. The largest snake is the reticulated python. The longest one ever found measured more than 30 feet (10 meters) long. This snake eats birds, rats, stray cats, goats, and even monkeys.

⇐ *Komodo dragons are the world's heaviest lizards. They hunt reptiles, wild pigs, and deer. They even eat their own young.*

⬇ *Saltwater crocodiles can swim far out to sea, hunting for prey to eat. Their massive jaws hold dagger-like teeth that can grow up to 5 inches (13 centimeters) long.*

ACTUAL ‹‹‹ SIZE ›››

Unlike its big cousins, the pygmy chameleon is just 1.4 inches(35 millimeters) long when fully grown, including its tail. Imagine how tiny it must be when it emerges from its egg!

Pygmy chameleon

in 1 2

17

Watch out!

Crocodiles and alligators can grow to a great size, even reaching 23 feet (7 meters) in length. Nile crocodiles normally hide underwater, waiting for their prey. They are so big and strong, with huge teeth and jaws, that they can attack and devour zebras and **wildebeest**.

Big Appetites

Animals that eat large meals often eat only occasionally, but those with smaller appetites spend most of their time feeding.

The no. 1 small to big **RECORD BREAKER** is the ...

SUNFISH

The sunfish grows up to 13 feet (4 meters) across, but a baby sunfish is smaller than a pea. This animal holds the record for the greatest difference in size between the adult and its young.

Gulper eels live in the ocean depths, where food is scarce. They grow to 6 feet (1.8 meters) long, but most of that is mouth! A gulper eel can open its jaws so wide that it can swallow a fish as big as itself. Its body stretches to fit the food in. The eel can last for weeks without another meal.

18

⇩ *The remains of this gulper eel's last meal can be seen as a bulge in its body.*

All mouth but no bite

Whale sharks are the biggest fish in the world. Their mouth can measure 60 inches (150 centimeters) across, but they don't use it to gobble up other marine monsters. Instead, they swim along with their mouth open, and water and small animals flow in. Their prey is mostly plankton—animals no bigger than your little finger.

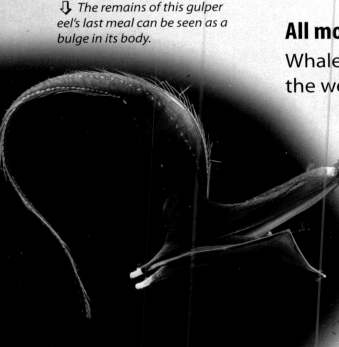

ACTUAL «« SIZE »»

Plankton are tiny animals and plants that float or swim in the ocean. Some are so small they can only be seen with a microscope. They are an important source of food for many other sea animals.

Plankton

⬆ *Whale sharks can grow to about 40 feet (12 meters) long. They spend most of their time swimming and feeding.*

Mighty Mates

At mating time, being big and strong can be a real advantage for male animals.

In many species, males have to fight one another to get a mate. The females choose males that look big, because it means they are more likely to have healthy young.

Fearsome horns

A male Hercules beetle can grow up to 7.5 inches (19 centimeters) long, including its huge horns. It uses these either for fighting rival males, or for scaring them away. The females are so much smaller that scientists once thought they belonged to a different species.

⇦ *Male Hercules beetles display their large horns to each other. The smaller one may decide to walk away from a fight.*

Shrinking male

Not all males outgrow their partners. Some grow into them! A male anglerfish is tiny and can sneak up on a female. He bites into her flesh and stays in place, to mate with her, for the rest of his life. His body gradually shrinks and he takes **nutrients** straight from her blood.

21

⇧ *In the deep, dark oceans, where anglerfish live, finding a mate is hard. So when a male anglerfish finally finds a female, he never lets go of her.*

ACTUAL «« SIZE »»

Hercules beetle

The horns of a Hercules beetle are made from a tough material called chitin. The top horn grows from the beetle's body and curves downward. The other one grows from its head and curves up. Together they look like huge biting jaws.

in   1   2   3   4

Body Bits

Why do animals grow strangely big, or small, body bits?

A body part may grow extra large if it has a very important job to do. Walruses, for example, have overgrown teeth, or tusks, which they dig into slippery ice to help pull themselves along. Male walruses also use their tusks to fight one another.

⇧ *Cavefish live in darkness, so they do not need to be able to see.*

Useless organs

Sometimes, a body part or **organ** may no longer be useful to an animal. Over time, the organ may shrink, or even disappear. Blind cavefish, for example, have either tiny eyes or no eyes at all.

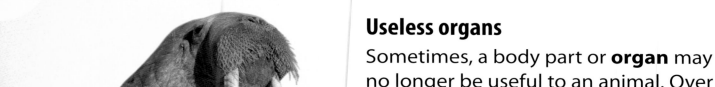

⇦ *The tusks of a walrus can be up over 3 feet (1 meter) long.*

⇨ *Tarsiers hunt at night. Their huge eyes help them find prey, such as insects, bats, birds, and snakes.*

Eyes like saucers

Animals that are active at night often have very big eyes, which give the animal better vision. The tarsier's eyes are huge in relation to its body size.

23

ACTUAL ⟪ SIZE ⟫

Dragonflies have eyes that take up most of their head. Each eye contains thousands of tiny lenses that produce a single image in the dragonfly's brain.

eye

Dragonfly

in 1   2   3

Marine Extremes

The oceans are home to the biggest and smallest of creatures.

The salt in the world's seas and oceans makes the water **dense**. This means it can support the weight of heavy animals, even if they don't have a bony skeleton—for example, octopuses and jellyfish.

⇩ *Blue whales spend the winter in cold polar waters, feasting on krill. They eat very little, or nothing at all, during the rest of the year.*

ACTUAL
««« SIZE »»»

Krill

Krill are small marine creatures that are closely related to prawns, crabs and lobsters. Billions of them can live in a single group, or swarm. Fish and whales travel long distances to feed on swarms of krill.

6   5   4   3   2   1

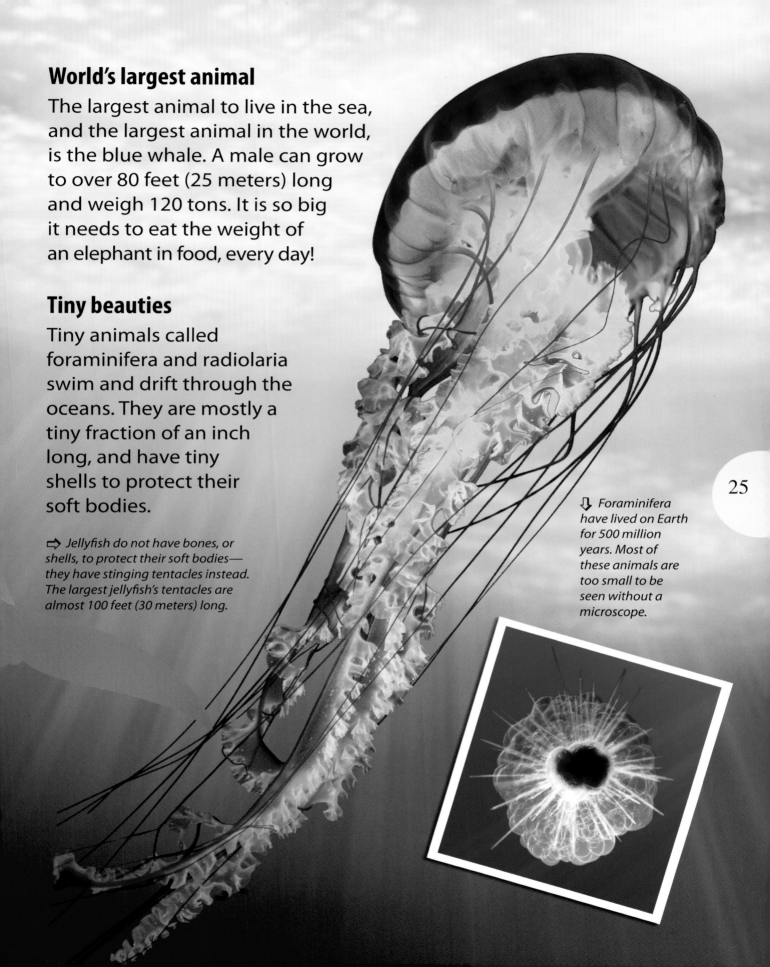

World's largest animal

The largest animal to live in the sea, and the largest animal in the world, is the blue whale. A male can grow to over 80 feet (25 meters) long and weigh 120 tons. It is so big it needs to eat the weight of an elephant in food, every day!

Tiny beauties

Tiny animals called foraminifera and radiolaria swim and drift through the oceans. They are mostly a tiny fraction of an inch long, and have tiny shells to protect their soft bodies.

⇨ *Jellyfish do not have bones, or shells, to protect their soft bodies— they have stinging tentacles instead. The largest jellyfish's tentacles are almost 100 feet (30 meters) long.*

⬇ *Foraminifera have lived on Earth for 500 million years. Most of these animals are too small to be seen without a microscope.*

Jungle Giants

Jungles, or tropical rainforests, are home to a huge range of living things of all shapes and sizes.

Rainforests are very special **habitats** that provide a home for lots of different species of living things because they offer plenty of food, shelter, water, and warmth. About 80 percent of all insect species live in rainforests.

Big and bold

When an immense Atlas moth flutters through the dappled shadows, it can easily be mistaken for a bird. Another jungle giant is the Philippine eagle, which is so vast and fast that it can catch a lemur as it leaps between trees.

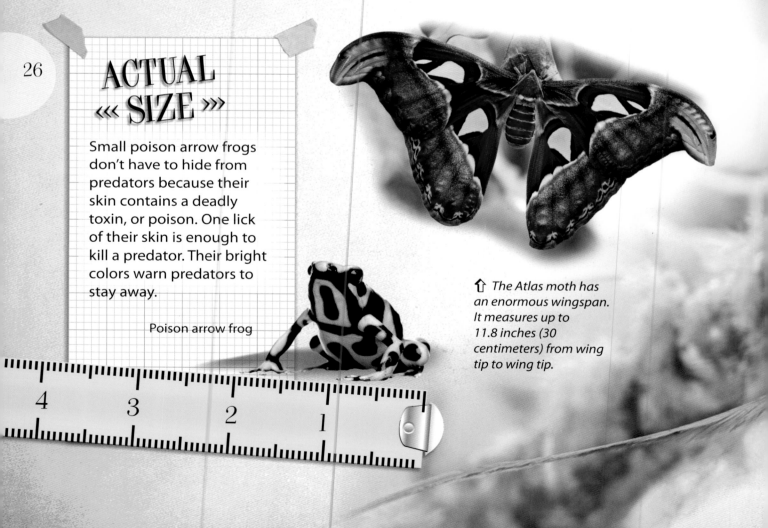

ACTUAL «« SIZE »»

Small poison arrow frogs don't have to hide from predators because their skin contains a deadly toxin, or poison. One lick of their skin is enough to kill a predator. Their bright colors warn predators to stay away.

Poison arrow frog

⇧ The Atlas moth has an enormous wingspan. It measures up to 11.8 inches (30 centimeters) from wing tip to wing tip.

4   3   2   1

Magnificent tail

Male quetzals catch the eye of possible mates by flashing their bold colors and tail feathers, which can reach over 3 feet (1 meter) long!

⇧ *The spiky feathers on a male quetzal's head are called a crest. Females do not have crests, or long tail feathers.*

Little Goes Large

In the big world of little animals, ganging up often works well. When they work together, animals can make mountains!

Tiny termites live in groups, or colonies, of up to five million. Their underground tunnels can extend 150 feet (45 meters) deep, and the mounds they make can be nearly 25 feet (7 meters) high.

⬇ *Termites are called social insects because they work together to build their enormous mounds. They feed on wood and plants, as well as fungi, which they grow inside the mound.*

The no. 1 animal structure **RECORD BREAKER** is ...

THE GREAT BARRIER REEF

Australia's Great Barrier Reef is the largest structure ever built by animals. It is more than 1,200 miles (2000 kilometers) long. The tiny **polyps** that are building it started work about 18 million years ago!

Safety in numbers

Red-billed queleas are the most numerous of all birds—there are billions of them in Africa. Queleas live in giant groups, called flocks, and this gives them protection from predators. When feeding on crops, a flock can strip whole fields in hours. One quelea flock may contain a million birds, or more.

⇦ *Red-billed queleas are small birds, but when they are flying in a giant flock they look like a dark storm cloud.*

⬇ *Honeybees are social insects. Up to 100,000 of them may live in a single nest.*

ACTUAL ‹‹‹ SIZE ›››

Honeybees on a honeycomb

Animals that live in colonies communicate with each other. Honeybees tell one another where to find the best flowers by performing a **waggle dance**!

in 1   2   3   4

Glossary

Air current Warm air is lighter than cool air, so it rises and moves across the sky. This is called an air current.

Animal kingdom The group of living things that contains all of the animals on Earth.

Complex animal An animal that has a body with limbs, such as legs or wings, and organs, such as a brain.

Dense Materials that are dense contain particles (tiny bits of stuff) that are closely packed together. Salty water is more dense than fresh water.

Habitat The place where an animal or plant lives.

Mammal An animal that has fur and feeds its young with milk.

Nutrient Found in food, nutrients contain the goodness that animals and plants need to live and grow.

Organ A part of the body that has a special job to do. The stomach, for example, digests food.

Polyp A soft-bodied animal that lives in the sea. It makes a stony substance around its body that collects and, over a long time, makes a coral reef.

Predator Any animal that hunts another animal to eat.

Primate A type of mammal with a large brain. Primates include humans, monkeys, and apes.

Species A type of animal or plant.

Tropical rainforest A warm forest where there is heavy rainfall all year long.

Venom A type of poison made by some animals, including various snakes, frogs, and spiders. Venom is used to kill prey or to cause pain to an attacker.

Wildebeest A kind of antelope, also known as a gnu.

Waggle dance Honeybees waggle their bodies, and walk around in circles. The way they do this 'waggle dance' shows other bees where to find flowers with sweet nectar to eat.

Index

Notes for Parents and Teachers

Here are some ideas for activities that adults and children can do together.

◆ The "Actual Size" panels will help children to understand many of the measurements in the book, but others need to be seen to be believed! Use a tape measure to explore the larger sizes quoted.

◆ Go on a bug hunt together. Gardens, parks, and woods offer lots of opportunities to watch insects and other invertebrates in their natural environment. Take a magnifying lens, a small ruler, a sketchbook, and a pencil to record your observations. Don't touch the bugs, though, and watch out for those that sting!

◆ Use weighing scales to find other things that weigh the same as a bee hummingbird.

◆ Many of the animals in this book can be seen in zoos and wildlife parks, or in natural history museums. If you are able to visit one of these places together, try and find the largest and smallest examples of types of animals. For example, find the largest cat or the smallest reptile.

◆ Encourage children to think how an animal's size might help the animal to find food or a mate, or avoid being eaten.

A TREE'S LIFE STORY

We can tell the age of a tree by the number of growth rings it has. Most trees grow a new layer of wood each year. Each layer makes another ring, which we can see when a tree is cut through. Some ancient bristlecone pines in North America have nearly 5,000 rings. The rings record hot, cold, and wet weather; pollution; and disease. Scientists can use them to learn about the climate and conditions of ancient times.

WHERE IN THE WORLD?

Because most land is found in the northern half of the world, most woodlands and forests are found here too. They lie between the cold Arctic and the hot, humid tropics. A band of coniferous forests runs across the north from Alaska to Siberia. Deciduous forests grow throughout North America, Europe, and Asia. Mixed woodlands grow in some of these areas, too. There are pockets of temperate rain forest in The United States, China, Japan, and New Zealand. Tropical rain forests grow near the Equator.

▶ In deciduous forests, the leaves on the trees lose their green color, dry out, and fall in autumn.

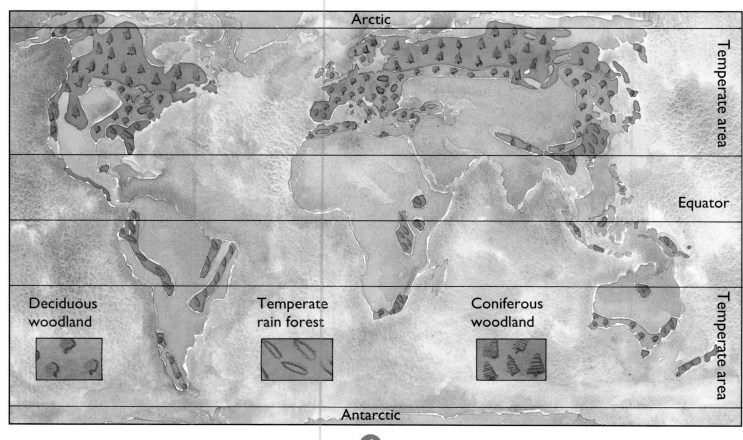

Arctic

Temperate area

Equator

Temperate area

Antarctic

Deciduous woodland

Temperate rain forest

Coniferous woodland

▲ The mountains in Colorado have mixed woodlands. Deciduous trees show their bright autumn colors, while snow covers the coniferous trees.

◀ Temperate rain forests have some of the world's tallest trees. Black bears, black-tailed deer, and the tiniest moles also live there.

Until a few hundred years ago, most of Europe and North America was covered with forest. People say that a squirrel could have crossed a whole **continent** without touching the ground. Today, only a fraction of that woodland is left. Much disappeared to make way for farming and building. The original **wildwoods** are now rare, although areas do still exist, for example in Poland, France, Great Britain, and North America.

SEASONAL CYCLES

Life in a woodland is always changing. In early spring, the days grow longer and warmer. **Migrating** birds arrive and build their nests. Flowers appear on the woodland floor. The first of the baby animals are born. They feed on the new green leaves so that they can grow strong before the cold weather comes. Sometimes animals have a second family to make sure that some young survive. When the summer comes, the forest buzzes with activity. Insects hatch, and woodland creatures feast on the nuts and fruits growing around them.

▲ The forest floor sometimes looks bare, because leaves and branches block out the light. Few plants can survive in the dark, shady area below.

◄ Most woodland flowers, such as these bluebells and red campions, bloom in late spring and early summer. They have to make the most of the sunlight to help them grow before the leaves on the trees open fully and cast a shadow over them. The range of species of flowers growing in an area of woodland can tell us about its age. Older woodlands often have a much wider variety than younger ones, and there are some species that can be found only in ancient woodlands.

Woodland creatures such as hedgehogs, dormice, and woodchucks hibernate through the winter. They curl up into a tight ball and stay fast asleep. Their bodies cool down to save energy. Squirrels, bears, and badgers doze during the cold months, waking and moving around from time to time. Squirrels nibble nuts they stored in the autumn.

The coats of some deer species change color with the seasons. This helps them to hide from **predators** when the landscape around them changes. An ermine's coat also changes, from brown in the summer to white in the winter.

Gradually the days grow shorter and colder. Trees prepare for the winter, changing color and then shedding their leaves. Animals grow thick coats and gather food that must last until spring. Some animals **hibernate** to escape the cold. Many species of birds migrate to warmer lands. Snow covers young plants like a blanket to protect them from frost. In the spring, the cycle begins again.

LEAF LIFE

Trees are a source of life for all the plants and animals in a woodland. They are **ecosystems** in themselves. The oak tree alone offers food and shelter to more than 300 species of insects. Most woodland trees grow from nuts that are spread by animals or, like other woodland plants, from seeds carried by the wind. This is why woodland flowers such as forget-me-nots are so small and hidden. They do not need to attract insects or birds to help them reproduce.

▶ American leaf-cutter ants take pieces of leaves into their nests. They use the leaves to fertilize the tiny fungus on which they feed.

LIFE IN A LOG

Nothing is wasted in a woodland. A fallen log lying on the forest floor gives food to other living things and is soon humming with new life. First the slugs and woodlice arrive. They are eaten by centipedes and spiders. A year or so later, fungi, mosses, and flowers coat the bark. Beetles chew into the wood, and reptiles such as lizards and snakes lie in wait for them. By the following year, hundreds of insects are busy laying eggs and storing food. Birds come to feed on them. Finally, the insects help the log to crumble, and it becomes part of the soil and helps new trees and other plants to grow.

Each species of tree grows best in a particular kind of soil and climate. Ancient oaks are at home in western Europe, as are beeches. These also grow in North America, along with giant redwoods and maples. In Russia and Canada, pines, larches, and other coniferous trees make up the biggest forests in the world. Massive kauri trees are native to New Zealand, where Maori people once made war canoes from them.

▲ The needles on a pine tree help it during the winter. When the ground is frozen, water cannot reach the trunk through the roots. Instead, the needles have a coating of wax that keeps the water inside them from escaping. The shape of the needles makes it difficult for snow to settle on the branches. Their dark color also helps them to absorb extra warmth from the sun.

▲ Many forest trees produce fruits and berries. These make a good meal for insects and birds such as the cedar waxwing of North America. People also eat some woodland fruits and can make use of every part of a tree, even the bark. Oak bark is sometimes used as a medicine for sore throats and nosebleeds, while witch hazel bark and leaves can soothe cuts and bruises.

FOREST BIRDS

Each woodland bird has its favorite niche or place in the forest. Eagles and hawks keep a lookout high in the branches. Owls and nuthatches peer out of old tree holes, and capercaillie rummage about on the forest floor. In spring, the forest hums with birdsongs from dawn to dusk. This is how birds claim their **territory** and attract a mate. Some give their mates a special **courtship display**. Waxwings give each other "presents," while male scarlet tanagers have bright, eye-catching red feathers.

Adult birds are always busy. They need to feed their chicks every few hours. Some have adapted especially to forest foods. Crossbills hook pine nuts out of cones with their unusual crossed-over beaks. Nutcrackers wedge nuts in crevices and drill out the kernel. They store nuts for the winter but sometimes forget where they left them. Woodpeckers eat ants in summer and pine nuts in winter. Nuthatches can hang upside down on tree trunks to catch insects. Sapsuckers trap insects in tree sap.

WINTER HOLIDAYS

Some birds migrate to escape the cold winter. Warblers steer by the stars to find their way, while thrushes follow the sun. Young cuckoos fly all the way to Africa without their parents. They all fly back again the following spring to build their nests.

◄ Woodpeckers use their beaks as high-speed drills to make holes in trees for nesting or hunting for food. They have very long, sticky tongues that they keep curled up inside their heads. When they have made a hole in the bark or wood of a tree, they reach their tongues inside and pick up insects.

▼ Tawny owls feed on mice and voles, which they catch from the forest floor and surrounding countryside. But they are under threat. Their woodland habitat has been destroyed in many places, forcing them to hunt in towns and near busy roads.

FOREST VEGETARIANS

Trees provide a larder for thousands of forest creatures. Insect **larvae** burrow into wood. Caterpillars chew leaf edges. Plant bugs suck tree sap. Deer, moose, rabbits, and hares munch new green shoots. In winter they eat nuts, berries, and bark, as do squirrels and wild boar. Worms and mites working deep in the forest floor transform dead leaves, which fall in the autumn, into new soil for the following spring.

▶ Beavers are expert engineers. They cut down whole trees with their sharp teeth to build dams and lodges in which to live. These homes have an underwater entrance to keep predators from getting in. Each part of the dam and lodge is built so that there will be no flooding.

FIGHTING FACTS

● Male deer fight "duels" in the breeding season. They use their antlers as weapons. The strongest one wins a whole herd of female deer with which to mate.

● When in danger, a squirrel can stay quite still for half an hour. It warns its family by thumping its feet and slapping its tail on the ground. If it is in a tree when an enemy is near, it drops down to a safe lower branch.

▶ Moose feed on leaves, tree shoots, twigs, and grasses. They have very soft, pliable lips and long muzzles that they use to delicately pick juicy leaves from high branches. They often bend young trees by pushing against the trunks as they reach up for the tender leaves growing at the top. They also eat plants from the bottom of forest lakes and prefer to live in swampy woodland areas.

▼ Chipmunks belong to the same family as squirrels. They burrow underground and build their nests in tunnels. Here they store food such as seeds and nuts that will last through their winter hibernation.

Many plant-eating woodland insects are very secretive in order to avoid predators. The female sawfly hides her eggs in pine needles. She slices the needles open with special "saws" on her legs and lays her eggs inside. Weevils roll up leaves into tubes and hide their eggs inside. Other insects disguise themselves to look like buds, bird droppings, twigs, or dead leaves to fool their enemies.

FOREST HUNTERS

Big forest **carnivores** are becoming rare. There are more of them in the coniferous forests of the north, because they are farther from the people who affect their woodland environment. Bears and wolves have suffered badly from the loss of large areas of forest, which have been cleared to make room for new buildings or farmland.

Lynx and wildcats sit high in the trees ready to pounce on small **rodents**. Wolves hunt together in packs for caribou, moose, and deer. They waste nothing and may bury leftovers for another day.

▼ Like badgers, wolves, and bats, foxes usually wait until dark to venture out of their dens to hunt. When cubs are a few weeks old, their mother takes them out for hunting lessons.

DID YOU KNOW?

● Some spiders trap their prey by wrapping it in a tight web.

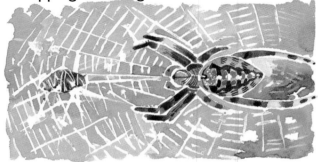

● A garden dormouse has a special safety device. If it is attacked, its tail can drop off, allowing it to escape with its life.

● Animals called gliding possums can "fly" from tree to tree using skin flaps that open like wings when they leap into the air.

● Shrews wait underground in tunnels for insects to fall through the entrance and then search them out with their snouts.

● When baby shrews are learning to hunt above ground, they stay together in a line. Each shrew holds the tail of the shrew in front of it in its mouth.

▲ Northern European forest dwellers such as the Lapp people herd reindeer as part of their traditional way of life. But now some of the forests where they spend the winter are threatened by logging companies.

◄ Bears love to eat fish. They wait in streams for salmon to leap out of the water. They also climb trees to raid insect nests in search of honey.

There were once many groups of **nomadic** forest people, such as **Native** Americans who hunted moose, deer, and beaver. A few still live as their ancestors did, but many were driven out by European settlers. The forests where they used to live are now being destroyed by developers who plan to exploit their **resources**.

WOODLAND RESOURCES

We all depend on the forest. In the north of the world, we use wood to make our lives comfortable. Many things that we use every day, from tables and chairs to pianos and guitars, begin as a tree. We turn wood into paper, then into books, newspapers, and packaging. Some of us use as many as 100 sheets of paper in a day. In the south of the world, wood is essential to survival. Half of all the trees cut down are used for fuel.

All sorts of fruits, nuts, seeds, and spices come from the world's forests.

Chestnuts and hazelnuts grow in deciduous woodlands. Apple, apricot, peach, and plum trees are traditional woodland species. Today, they are cultivated, and the fruits are sold fresh or dry. The sap from maple trees makes maple syrup.

However, even with all these products, we take very little food from the forest compared to the quantity of wood we use.

▼ This Gambian woman carries home a supply of wood, which she will burn to provide heat, cook food, and heat water.

CORK FACTS

Cork comes from the bark of the cork oak tree. It is stripped off only once every 10 years to allow the tree to grow a new layer. When the bark is dry it is processed to make floor tiles and corks for bottles.

▲ Paper comes from coniferous trees like the spruce, pine, and larch. Millions of these trees are cut down every year. The wood is chopped up, pulped, mixed with water, and spread out to dry. It is then used to make newsprint, books, packaging, and other paper products.

▲ The simple pine tree gives us pine nuts, paper, glue, and perfumes.

In addition to being an important resource for people, woodlands house millions of unique plants and animals. They also hold soil in place so it does not wash away. They provide moisture for rain, and they help to keep our climate in balance.

SHRINKING WOODLANDS

It is not just tropical rain forests that are disappearing today. Ancient woodlands are going too. In Canada, two-thirds of the forests have already vanished. In North America, only 1 tree in every 20 is spared.

Half of Britain's wildwoods have disappeared in the last century. Beavers, bears, and lynx went with them. In Scandinavia, many of the newly planted forests contain only one tree species.

Trees are cut down to make way for homes, farming, and industry. Some are destroyed by forest fires, others by storms. "Acid rain" caused by factory fumes kills trees and pollutes the soil, rivers, and lakes. Germany's white fir trees have been damaged in this way. Hunting, too, endangers animals. For example, there are very few bison left living wild in the world today.

The results are serious. Rare plants and animals are losing their habitats. Soil is **eroding**, climate patterns are changing, and droughts and floods are increasing as the world gradually heats up. We need to act now. Our future depends on it.

DID YOU KNOW?

● When logging companies cut down trees in North America, a quarter of them are not used and are left on the ground to rot.

● Since 1950, over half the world's trees have disappeared, and many species are now under threat.

● We are losing nearly 70 species of wildlife every day. Not since the time of the dinosaurs have so many unique species disappeared every day. At present rates of extinction, as much as a third of the world's species could be gone by the year 2020.

SAVING OUR WOODLANDS

All over the world, people are working to protect woodlands and their wildlife. Environmental groups are campaigning to save endangered species. The sable used to be killed for its hair, which was used to make paintbrushes. Happily, it has been saved from **extinction**. National Parks in many places allow animals to live and breed in peace. People are not allowed to hunt or light fires in these areas.

We need to take even better care of our woodlands. In Sweden and Finland, more trees are planted than cut down. But only one or two species are planted, so the wildlife is suffering. It needs a variety of trees to make up its true habitat. If we doubled the amount of paper we recycle, we could reduce by half the number of trees we cut down. This would help to preserve the rich, ancient forests that remain. Governments need to take urgent action to reduce pollution and prevent further **deforestation** and loss of species. They could also encourage **conservation**.

▲ Some Hindus in parts of India hold special ceremonies in which they offer gifts to trees to show their respect for nature and living things.

◄ Tree-planting programs are being set up in every country. These children in Sri Lanka are taking seedlings to a tree nursery to plant.

The Chipko Movement was started by a group of Indian women who saved their forest from loggers by hugging the trees. When the axemen came, the women surrounded the trunks and refused to move. They explained how the trees prevent the soil from eroding and help to keep the rivers flowing. The government agreed to stop the logging.

WHAT YOU CAN DO

● Join a conservation group. Support its work, find out more, and even help to protect a rare bird or animal.

● Collect a few acorns and conkers in the autumn. Plant them in your yard, at school, or in a patch of wasteland. Take care of them and watch them grow.

● Start a paper-recycling or tree-planting program at school or where you live.

● Encourage your family to buy environment-friendly and recycled products.

BOMBO MEETS MOTHER EAGLE

For thousands of years people have told stories about the world around them. Often these stories try to explain something that people do not understand. This tale is told by the Iroquois people of the forests of the Eastern United States.

Bombo was a great hunter. He lived deep in the forests of Pennsylvania and caught more deer than any hunter his people had ever known. Every morning he set out with his special green bow and his long, sharp arrows. Every lunchtime he returned with a deer slung over his shoulder.

Bombo had magic power. All he had to do was call to the deer, and they would come and graze near his home. But he was not satisfied. He wanted more.

One day he decided to test his power. He called to the eagles, "Hey, Eagles, I have fresh meat here for you. Come and take it to your aeries." Golden eagles swooped down from all directions. There were males, females, and even some young ones who had only just learned to fly. But as they reached the feast, Bombo shot them one by one and stole their feathers.

The next day, Bombo called the eagles again. Eighteen female birds glided majestically down to find food for their chicks. He aimed his arrow and was just about to shoot when a voice behind him said, "Stop!" Bombo swung around in surprise. Standing before him was his best friend, Lilo.

"This is very dangerous, Bombo," he warned. "You must stop immediately. The animals are upset and angry. It is wrong to shoot the eagles and take their feathers."

"Nonsense," replied Bombo. "I'm not doing any harm. Look at my beautiful feather collection. I can make some amazing arrows now."

"You're wrong," said Lilo. "I'm your friend, and I don't want to see you hurt, but if you don't stop, the animals will teach you a lesson."

But Bombo ignored his friend and walked off, shaking his head.

The next day Bombo called the eagles for the third time. To his surprise, nothing happened. The forest remained silent and still. As Bombo strained his ears for some sound from the eagles, he thought that he could hear a faint humming. Suddenly, a gigantic dark shape loomed out of the sky toward him. It was the mother of all eagles – and she was very, very angry. Bombo had never been so terrified in his life. He took one look at her and ran off as fast as he could. He spotted a hollow log and quickly wriggled inside, but Mother Eagle was just behind him. She grabbed him with her huge claws and swept him up into the air with two angry beats of her powerful wings.

They flew up and up until the forest looked like a green carpet below them. Bombo's heart was beating faster and faster. He felt dizzy. The forest seemed to turn from green to blue. Mother Eagle swooped up and down and around in circles until Bombo thought he would die. As they soared up again, he thought he glimpsed the edge of the forest way below. He panicked. Were they about to leave his home altogether?

All of a sudden, they were heading straight for a huge tree. Just as Bombo was sure they were going to crash, Mother Eagle swooped down into her aerie, dropped him into her nest with her chicks, and flew off.

Bombo was terrified. How would he get home now? Suddenly he had an idea. In his pocket he had some dried meat and leather thongs. He offered the meat to the eaglets, who gobbled it up greedily, then he tied their beaks with the thongs.

When Mother Eagle came back with food for her chicks and saw what Bombo had done, she was furious.

"This is wrong, Bombo. Untie them this minute," she cried.

"No," replied Bombo. "I won't untie them until you promise to let me go."

For two days Mother Eagle tried to unpick the tight leather thongs with her sharp beak, but to no avail. Meanwhile, her chicks grew thinner and thinner. They were soon so weak that they could hardly stand up. Mother Eagle flew off around the forest with a grave look on her face.

Finally, she returned to the nest.

"I'll make a pact with you, Bombo," she said. "If you promise never to kill another eagle without permission from the Spirit World, and if you untie my chicks this minute, you may safely go back to your home."

"I promise," he replied, untying the thongs so that the hungry chicks could eat at last. As Mother Eagle fed her family, Bombo saw them grow big and strong right before his eyes. Suddenly, before he could even blink, he found himself back, safe and sound, in his own home.

From that day on, whenever Bombo caught a deer, he called the eagles and invited them to come and share the meal in safety. He never killed another eagle, and the only feathers he collected were the ones the eagles left for him. From then on, all the hunters in the forest followed Bombo's example. The eagles and the forest people understood one another at last.

TRUE OR FALSE?

Which of these facts are true and which ones are false?
If you have read this book carefully, you will know the answers.

1. Most woodlands are in the top half of the world.

2. Beavers warn their families of trouble by thumping their feet and slapping their tails.

3. Ermines have a white coat in summer and a brown coat in winter.

4. Nuthatches stand upside down on tree trunks to catch insects.

5. A woodpecker has such a long tongue that it has to keep it curled up inside its head.

6. Waxwings have bright red feathers to attract a mate.

7. If a wolf is attacked, its tail can drop off to allow it to escape.

8. Indian women saved their forest by hugging the trees.

9. Rabbits have special skin flaps so that they can fly through the forest.

10. Maori people used pine trees to make war canoes.

GLOSSARY

● **Carnivore** An animal that eats other animals to survive. An herbivore only eats plants. An omnivore eats both meat and plants.

● **Coniferous forest** A forest made up of evergreen trees, which have cones and needles.

● **Conservation** The protection and preservation of wildlife and the environment in which it lives.

● **Courtship display** When a bird, animal, or insect performs or changes color to attract a mate.

● **Continent** One of the world's large land masses, usually divided into a number of countries.

● **Deciduous forest** A forest made up of trees that lose their leaves in winter.

● **Deforestation** Destroying large areas of woodland to make room for building, mining, or farming.

● **Ecosystem** A community of plants and animals and its environment.

● **Eroding** The wearing away of soil or land by wind or water. Trees help to prevent erosion.

● **Evergreens** Trees and plants that have green leaves all year around.

● **Extinction** When a species dies out completely, it is said to be extinct.

● **Habitat** The natural environment of a plant or animal.

● **Hibernate** To sleep during the winter. While hibernating, animals use very little energy, and many do not need food.

● **Larvae** The young of some insect species before they develop and grow wings.

● **Migrate** To travel long distances every year. Many birds migrate from their summer breeding grounds to warmer winter feeding places.

● **Mixed woodlands** Forests with evergreen trees as well as seasonal deciduous trees.

● **Native** A plant, animal, or person whose family originally comes from the area in which it lives.

● **Nomadic** People who move from place to place in search of pasture and food are nomadic.

● **Predator** An animal that hunts and kills other creatures.

● **Rain forest** A thick, evergreen forest with high levels of rainfall. Temperate rain forests are warm and moist with most rainfall in winter. Tropical rain forests are hot and wet with heavy rainfall all year around.

● **Resources** Natural materials, such as wood, taken from their environment and used by people.

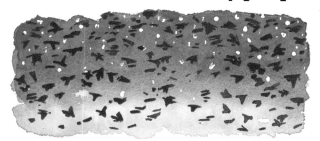

● **Rodent** A small mammal, such as a squirrel or beaver, with strong front teeth that it uses for gnawing hard objects.

● **Species** A group of animals or plants that shares the same characteristics and can breed with one another.

● **Territory** The area where an animal lives and breeds.

● **Woodland** An area of land in temperate countries, where many trees grow close together.

● **Wildwoods** Ancient woodlands in their natural state, inhabited by their original species.

INDEX

RESOURCES

Enter the World of the Woodlands: Panorama Book and Sticker Sets, by Scott Sonneborn, Garen Baker, 1995. Boldly colored introduction to the North American woodlands and the fascinating creatures that live there. Each animal in the book has its own reusable vinyl sticker to place in two beautiful foldout woodland environments.

Forests and Woodlands, by Rose Pipes, 1998. Introduces some notable forests and woodlands around the world, including the taiga in Russia, the eucalyptus woodlands in Australia, and the mangrove forests of Central and South America.

Temperate Forest Mammals, by Elaine Landau, 1996. This book introduces children ages 5-8 to five animals that make their home in this environment: beavers, echidnas, raccoons, koalas, and wild boars.